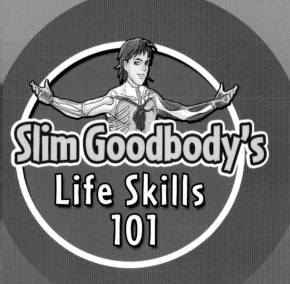

Slim Goodbody's Life Skills 101

SPEAK UP!

Communicating Confidently

CRABTREE
Publishing Company
www.crabtreebooks.com

Crabtree Publishing Company
www.crabtreebooks.com

Series Development, Writing, and Packaging:
John Burstein, Slim Goodbody Corp.

Editors:
Lynn Peppas
Valerie Weber, Wordsmith Ink.

Editorial director:
Kathy Middleton

Production coordinator:
Ken Wright

Prepress technician:
Ken Wright

Designer:
Tammy West, Westgraphix LLC.

Photos:
Chris Pinchbeck, copyright, Pinchbeck Photography

Photo credits:
© iStock Photos: pages 4 (bottom), 6 (top), 17 (top), 18, 23
© Shutterstock: page 13
© Slim Goodbody: pages 1, 2, 4 (top), 6 (bottom), 7, 8, 9, 10, 11, 12, 14, 15, 16, 17 (bottom), 18 (bottom), 19, 20, 21, 22, 23 (bottom), 24, 25, 26, 27, 28, 29

Acknowledgements:
The author would like to thank the following people for their help in this project:
Christine Burstein, Lucas Burstein, Tristan Fong, Jessie Goodale, Adriana Goodale, Colby Hill, Ginny Laurita, Louis Laurita, Renaissance Lyman, Jack Henry Grannis-Phoenix, Ariel Power, Joah Welt

"Slim Goodbody" and Pinchback photos, copyright, © Slim Goodbody

"Slim Goodbody" and "Slim Goodbody's Life Skills 101" are registered trademarks of the Slim Goodbody Corp.

Library and Archives Canada Cataloguing in Publication

Burstein, John
    Speak up! : communicating confidently / John Burstein.

(Slim Goodbody's life skills 101)
Includes index.
Issued also in an electronic format.
ISBN 978-0-7787-4797-0 (bound).--ISBN 978-0-7787-4813-7 (pbk.)

    1. Interpersonal communication--Juvenile literature.
2. Assertiveness (Psychology)--Juvenile literature. I. Title.
II. Title: Communicating confidently. III. Series: Burstein, John.
Slim Goodbody's life skills 101.

BF637.C45B88 2011   j153.6   C2010-902820-1

Library of Congress Cataloging-in-Publication Data

Burstein, John.
  Speak up! : communicating confidently / [John Burstein].
    p. cm. -- (Slim Goodbody's life skills 101)
  Includes index.
  ISBN 978-0-7787-4813-7 (pbk. : alk. paper) -- ISBN 978-0-7787-4797-0
(reinforced library binding : alk. paper) -- ISBN 978-1-4271-9535-7
(electronic (pdf)
  1. Interpersonal communication--Juvenile literature. 2. Assertiveness (Psychology)
--Juvenile literature. 3. Interpersonal communication in children--Juvenile
literature. 4. Assertiveness in children--Juvenile literature. I. Title. II. Series.

  BF637.C45B874 2011
  153.6--dc22
                               2010016767

Crabtree Publishing Company
www.crabtreebooks.com   1-800-387-7650

Printed in Hong Kong/042011/BK20110304

Published in Canada
Crabtree Publishing
616 Welland Ave.
St. Catharines, Ontario
L2M 5V6

Published in the United States
Crabtree Publishing
PMB 59051
350 Fifth Avenue, 59th Floor
New York, New York 10118

Published in the United Kingdom
Crabtree Publishing
Maritime House
Basin Road North, Hove
BN41 1WR

Published in Australia
Crabtree Publishing
386 Mt. Alexander Rd.
Ascot Vale (Melbourne)
VIC 3032

CONTENTS

SPEAKING THE TRUTH.............................4

PASSING THE WORDS 6

LOSE-WIN.............................8

WIN-LOSE.............................10

WIN-WIN.............................12

LET'S COMPARE.............................14

STEP BY STEP.............................16

STEP 3: FOCUS ON FEELINGS.............................18

STEP 4: "I" STATEMENTS.............................20

TRY THE "I".............................22

STEP 7: LEARN TO LISTEN,
      LISTEN TO LEARN.............................24

STEP 9: ACCEPT RESPONSIBILITY.............................26

THINK WIN-WIN.............................28

GLOSSARY.............................30

FOR MORE INFORMATION.............................31

INDEX.............................32

Words in **bold** are defined in the glossary on page 30.

SPEAKING THE TRUTH

Blake's doorbell rang. It was his next-door neighbor Jacob. "Hi Blake," Jacob greeted him. "Can I borrow your soccer ball?" Jacob was always borrowing stuff. One day, it would be a book and the next day, a DVD or a game.

Blake usually didn't mind lending his things to people. But Jacob was different. He always forgot to return the things he borrowed. Blake would have to go over Jacob's house and ask for his stuff back. Sometimes Jacob couldn't find it. Sometimes Jacob had damaged it. There was always some kind of problem to deal with.

Blake believed that if you borrow something, you should return it on time and in good condition. He wanted to tell Jacob this, but he couldn't figure out how to say it. Blake wasn't afraid of Jacob. He just didn't want to hurt his feelings or to sound mean.

"Well, I don't know," Blake said.

"C'mon, Blake, be a pal," said Jacob. "I'll bring it back in an hour."

Blake wanted to say, "No way. In an hour, my ball will be lost, ruined, or forgotten." Instead he just replied, "OK, I guess you can have it."

"Thanks, Blake, you're great," Jimmy said happily.

After Jimmy left, Blake felt really upset. He thought, "Jimmy's happy, and I feel crummy! Maybe next time, I'll tell him the way I really feel."

Hi. My name is Slim Goodbody.

I'll bet that most of you have had conversations that left you feeling **frustrated**. Maybe you couldn't find the right words. Or maybe you just didn't feel comfortable speaking your mind.

There may have been many reasons for this. For example, you might have felt

- afraid of hurting someone's feelings;

- afraid that somebody would get mad at you;

- that you had no right to say no;

- uncertain about how to ask for what you wanted.

Luckily there is a **communication** skill you can learn. This skill is called **assertive** communication. Assertive communication means expressing your thoughts, feelings, and needs clearly and honestly.

PASSING THE WORDS

Communication is how you share ideas with other people. When communication is good, it allows you to

- gather information about your world;
- express your needs and wants;
- ask for help;
- build trusting **relationships**;
- figure out solutions to problems.

A Matter of Style

Everyone has a different style, or way of doing things. For example, someone's style may be to get his homework finished as soon as he gets home. Someone else's style might be to play outside first and do homework after dinner. People have different styles in the way they dress, dance, and play sports. Scientists have also discovered people use one of three styles when they communicate.

Suppose two people are trying to decide what to do. They might use one of the following styles when discussing their **options**:

- Passive. For example, someone who uses a **passive** style might say, "I'll do whatever you want to do. I don't care." But the person may actually have feelings or **opinions**. The person just isn't expressing them.

- **Aggressive.** Someone who uses an **aggressive** style might say, "You have to do what I want or you're going to get it!"

- **Assertive.** Someone who uses an assertive style might say, "I would rather do something I want to do right now. Maybe we could do what you want afterward."

Most people use all three styles from time to time, but every person usually has one style he or she uses more than any other.

It's a Habit

Sometimes styles or habits need to be broken. First, however, you need to know what your habit is.

You're probably not sure what communication style you use. After all, you can't just look in a mirror and see a sign above your head that says "Passive **Communicator**," "**Aggressive** Communicator," or "Assertive Communicator." To find your main style, let's look closer at each of the three communication styles.

LOSE-WIN

A person who uses the passive communication style might say, "I'll go along with whatever you want to do." At first, you might think this is a pretty good way to communicate. It sounds relaxed, friendly, and helpful. If you truly don't care one way or another about something, it's fine to just go along.

However, if you use passive communication instead of saying how you really feel, that can be a problem. Passive communication sends a message to others that

- your thoughts and feelings aren't as important as theirs;
- it's OK to ignore your wants and needs;
- you are ready to give in, whether you agree with something or not.

Passive communicators believe, "I lose. You win."

Peacekeepers

People often use a passive communication style to avoid **conflicts** with others. Passive communicators don't want to upset anyone, so they don't object to something when they might want to. Passive communicators try to "keep the peace," even when it means keeping their thoughts and feelings secret. They believe that telling their real feelings will hurt someone else's feelings.

POP!

Keeping your feelings hidden doesn't make those feelings disappear. You may avoid a conflict on the outside, but there's trouble brewing within. For example, some people hold in their anger. Day after day, it builds up inside until someone or something sets it off. Then boom—the anger explodes! People who bottle up their feelings often end up yelling at others in angry, hurtful ways.

Check Yourself Out!

Think about it. You probably have a passive communication style if most of the following statements are true for you:

- You hold in your feelings rather than risk upsetting others.

- You believe that other peoples' needs are more important than yours.

- You think that if you speak up, others will just ignore you.

- You often get upset with yourself for not speaking up.

WIN-LOSE

People with an aggressive communication style like to boss others around. They tend to yell if they don't get their way.

Aggressive communicators look like know-it-alls or bullies. They do not respect the feelings and rights of others. They don't try to see **situations** from another's point of view. They want to win at all costs. Aggressive communicators believe, "I win. You lose."

What's Wrong with Getting What You Want?

You may think that an aggressive style works well because it gets you what you want. However, getting your way all the time often makes other people angry with you. People may do what you want, but they don't feel happy about it. They will **resent** you, not respect you. People will tend to avoid you and not want to be your friend.

A Self-Check

Check yourself out. You probably have an aggressive communication style if most of the following statements are true for you:

- You put your own needs first all the time.

- You often speak in a loud voice.

- You are pushy and bullying.

- You usually insist on getting your own way.

- You don't pay attention to other people's opinions.

- You scare, threaten, or blame others.

WIN-WIN

Assertive communication is based upon respect for each other. People who use assertive communication assume the best about people. They believe that both sides in a conflict want the right solution for everyone. When you use assertive communication, you state your point of view clearly and strongly. However, you are also willing to listen to what someone else has to say about a conflict. You are open to change, hoping to find a solution that fits everyone's needs. Assertive communicators believe, "I win AND you win too."

You Can't Always Get What You Want

Respecting other people's opinions means that sometimes you can get what you want and other times you won't. When you listen to others, you may find that your opinion about something is wrong. Other times, someone might listen to your opinion and discover that you were right and they were wrong.

Powerful Benefits

Using assertive communication can help you and others in many ways. For example, assertive communication

- allows you the freedom to express your thoughts, needs, and feelings openly;
- **promotes** respect for the thoughts, needs, and feelings of others;
- encourages you to stand up for your rights and for the rights of others;
- earns you respect from others because they know that you are honest;
- increases your good feelings about yourself;
- sets an example and inspires others to communicate clearly;
- helps everyone get their needs met;
- helps you create better relationships;
- reduces the chance of hurt feelings;
- reduces stress caused by **misunderstandings** and conflicts.

The goal of assertive communication isn't to "get your own way" all the time. It isn't about "giving up and giving in" all the time either. The goal is to increase understanding and honest sharing.

LET'S COMPARE

Now that we've discussed all three communication styles, let's take another look at how they compare.

Assertive

Message: My rights count, and so do yours.

Outcome: I win, you win

Passive

Message: Your rights count, mine don't

Outcome: I lose, you win

COMMUNICATION STYLES

Aggressive

Message: My rights count, yours don't

Outcome: I win, you lose

Let's Look at Life

Let's think about some real-life situations. They will help you see the differences among the three ways of communicating.

1. Someone cuts in front of you in line.

A passive communicator would just let the person push in. Perhaps he might mumble something like, "Go ahead. It's fine with me."

An aggressive communicator might angrily say, "Hey, loser, no cuts!"

An assertive communicator might assume that the person didn't see him in line. He would politely say, "Excuse me, but I was in line."

2. Your friend loves to talk. You have a lot of homework to do, however, and don't have time to chat.

A passive communicator would just let the friend talk for as long as she needs. She would make up the time by staying up late to get her homework done.

An aggressive communicator might become angry that her friend doesn't respect her time. She might say, "Why can't you leave me alone for awhile? You're always bothering me."

An assertive communicator will listen for a minute or two. Then she'll tell her friend, "I'd love to talk to you, but I don't have the time right now. Can we talk later tonight?"

STEP BY STEP

You can learn how to be an assertive communicator. All it takes is following a series of steps and practicing as you go along.

Step 1: A "You View"

Before you can move ahead, you need to know where you stand right now. The first step is to take an honest look at yourself—a "you view." Figure out how you usually communicate. Ask yourself the following questions. The answers will help clue you in about your communication style.

- Do I keep quiet most of the time? (You're probably a passive communicator.)

- Do I go along with others just to avoid disappointing them? (Again, probably a passive communicator)

- Do I push other people around and make them do what I want? (Probably an aggressive communicator)

- Do I spend a lot of time blaming other people? (Aggressive communicator)

- Do people seem afraid to talk to me, especially when I disagree with them? (Aggressive communicator)

- Do I feel hurt and attacked when someone expresses a different opinion than mine? (Passive communicator)

If you answered yes to any one of these questions, you may benefit from learning assertive communication skills.

Second Opinion

If you are having trouble answering these questions, get a second opinion. Ask a classmate or family member what they think. Promise them you will not get mad, no matter what they say. Otherwise they may be afraid to speak the truth.

Step 2: Know When

Think carefully about recent situations. Were there times you felt you didn't communicate very well? For example, did they happen

- when you were arguing with a friend;
- when somebody asked you to do something you didn't want to do;
- when somebody left you out of a game?

Write down a list of these situations. Knowing where you need to improve your communication skills can inspire you to make changes.

Now you're ready for step 3.

STEP 3: FOCUS ON FEELINGS

When you use assertive communication, you let others know how you are feeling. People then have information about what's bothering you.

But before you can share your feelings, you need to figure out what those feelings are. As strange as it may sound, many people are confused about what they actually feel. To help you gain a better understanding of your feelings, ask yourself questions like:

- What makes me angry or sad?
- What makes me feel worried or upset?
- What makes me happy?
- What kind of feelings do I have a lot of and which do I have a little?

Think Back

It may be helpful to remember recent events in your life. Think about how they made you feel. For example, you might think, "I felt sad when my friend didn't play with me." Or, "I felt angry when my brother played a trick on me."

Give yourself time. Learning to tune in to your feelings takes practice.

Expand Your Vocabulary

The more you can identify your feelings, the more you will understand them. Practice using the exact word to describe your feeling at any given time. For example:

- Did someone *annoy* you or make you *furious*?
- Did something someone said *surprise* you, or were you *shocked*?
- Did a gift make you *happy*, or did you feel *ecstatic*?

Write Those Feelings Down

When you are writing, your mind doesn't drift off easily. If you can't put a feeling into words, you can draw it! Then you can go back and study your feelings in greater depth or add more details. Writing things down can also help you plan how you might handle different situations. When you have a better understanding of your feelings, you're ready to move on the next step.

STEP 4: "I" STATEMENTS

You may really want to tell people that they did wrong. For example, you might want to say:

- "You were mean to me."
- "You made me mad!"
- "You hurt my feelings."

Statements that begin with "You" sound like you're blaming another person.

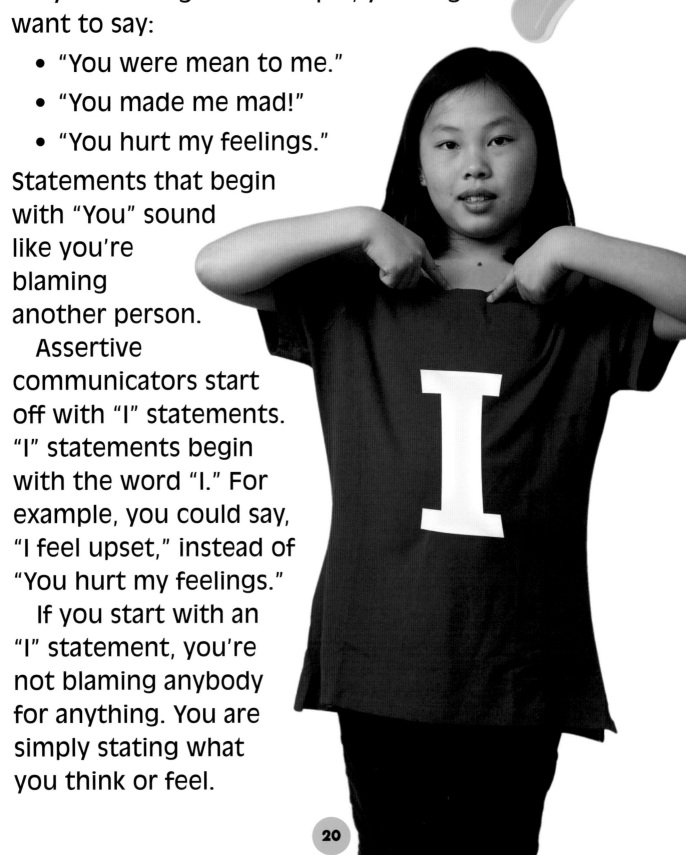

Assertive communicators start off with "I" statements. "I" statements begin with the word "I." For example, you could say, "I feel upset," instead of "You hurt my feelings."

If you start with an "I" statement, you're not blaming anybody for anything. You are simply stating what you think or feel.

A Four-Part Formula

Starting with "I" is just the beginning. You need to follow it up with a more complete description of what you're feeling and thinking. You might find this four-part formula helpful:

I feel _____ when _____
because _____ I need _____.

1. "I feel _____" Express how you feel about the other person's behavior. For example, "I feel angry" or "I feel hurt." Remember the vocabulary you practiced in Step 3.

2. "When _____" What bothers you about a behavior or situation? For example, "When my friends call me 'stupid.'"

3. "Because _____" How does the behavior affect you? For example, "Because I feel bad about myself."

4. "I need _____" State what you want to change. For example, "I need you to stop calling me names."

Knowing what you need allows others to make changes and fix the problem. While this formula will not work all the time, it will help in most situations.

It takes practice to create a strong, four-part "I" statement. Practicing with the adults in your family can be helpful. Here are some models to help you make up your own "I" statements:

- "I feel upset when people make fun of me, because teasing hurts my feelings. I need you to stop making fun of me.

- "I feel angry when you don't return what you borrowed, because I got it for my birthday. I need you to give it back now."

- "I feel frustrated when you come late, because we miss the start of the movie. I need you to come on time from now on.

Step 5: Speak with Confidence

What you say is very important. So is how you say it. When you use assertive communication, always try to speak in a strong and confident tone of voice. People need to hear you clearly. Yelling can be way too aggressive. Whispering can be way too passive.

Step 6: Body Language

The way you hold your body, or your **body language**, actually communicates information about you. You don't have to say a word! Suppose you are hunched over and looking down. Your body language communicates that you are sad or upset. Assertive communication also involves using the correct body language.

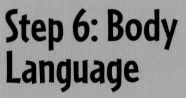

Assertive Communicators

- stand up straight to show their confidence;
- lean forward a bit to show their interest;
- keep a pleasant expression on their face to show they are calm;
- look people in the eye to show that they are paying attention;
- relax their shoulders to show they are not nervous.

STEP 7: LEARN TO LISTEN, LISTEN TO LEARN

Assertive communicators are not afraid to listen. They understand that the point of communication is understanding, not winning. The only way to gain understanding is to listen to what the other person has to say.

When you listen, you show respect. Listening also lets others know that you are interested in finding out their side of the story. If you listen to others, they are far more likely to listen to you in return. When you are listening to someone, keep these tips in mind:

- Don't assume you know what the other person is thinking and feeling. The only way you can find out this kind of information is when they tell you.

- Try to imagine you are inside the other person's mind and seeing things from her point of view.

- Focus on what is being said and not on what you are going to say when the other person stops talking.
- Try not to interrupt. If you do not understand something, though, ask questions.

Keep in mind that understanding someone is different from agreeing with them. Someone can tell you something that you will never agree with, but you can still listen.

Step 8: Control Your Temper

When you disagree with someone, it's natural to feel angry. But anger can crowd out clear thinking and common sense. If you lose your temper, you may end up arguing instead of communicating. While you are listening and speaking, it's important to control your temper.

Assertive communicators know when to take a break. Suppose you are in the middle of a conversation. You feel yourself or your partner starting to get too angry. Take time to cool off. When you feel ready and in control, start the conversation again.

STEP 9: ACCEPT RESPONSIBILITY

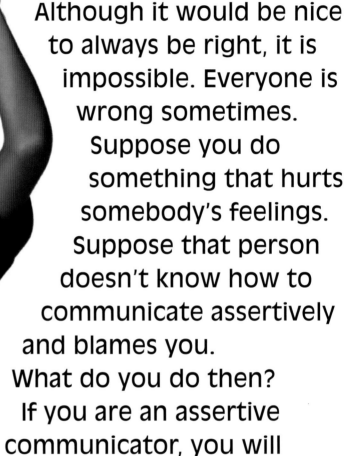

Although it would be nice to always be right, it is impossible. Everyone is wrong sometimes. Suppose you do something that hurts somebody's feelings. Suppose that person doesn't know how to communicate assertively and blames you.
What do you do then?
If you are an assertive communicator, you will

• take responsibility for your behavior and apologize. Taking responsibility means that you admit you made a mistake. Admitting responsibility for doing something wrong shows strength, not weakness.

• respect the other person's feelings.

• try to come up with a fair solution to the problem.

• continue to believe in yourself. Say to yourself, "Just because I made a mistake, I am still a good person."

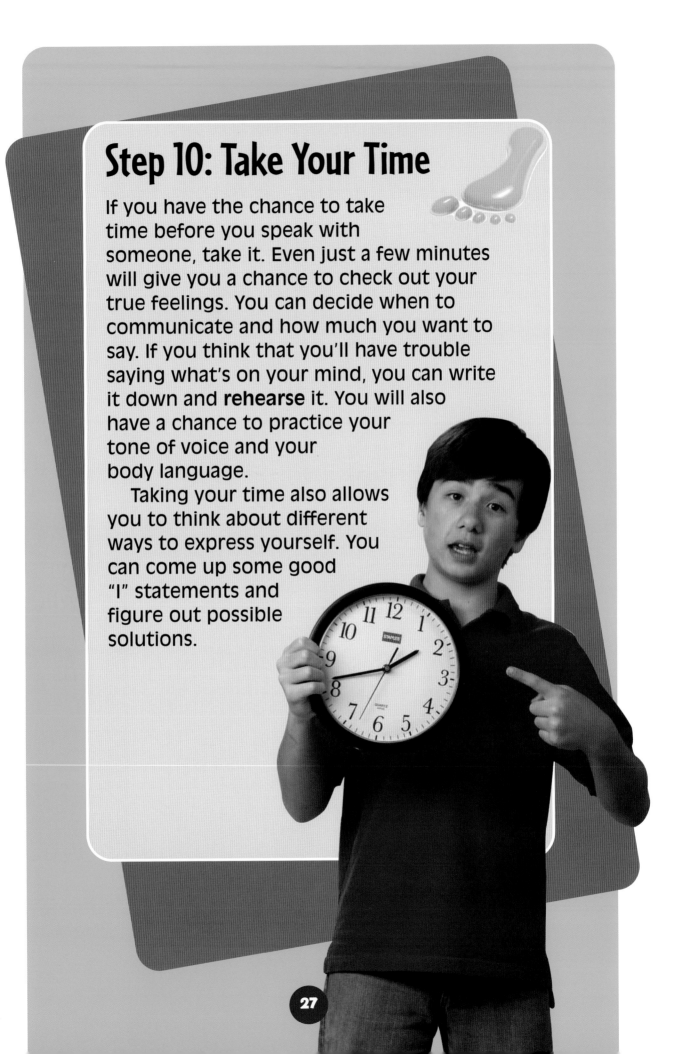

Step 10: Take Your Time

If you have the chance to take time before you speak with someone, take it. Even just a few minutes will give you a chance to check out your true feelings. You can decide when to communicate and how much you want to say. If you think that you'll have trouble saying what's on your mind, you can write it down and **rehearse** it. You will also have a chance to practice your tone of voice and your body language.

Taking your time also allows you to think about different ways to express yourself. You can come up some good "I" statements and figure out possible solutions.

THINK WIN-WIN

Assertive communicators try to always think win-win. Instead of trying to just get what they want, they look for solutions that meet everybody's needs.

Know Your Rights

It doesn't matter what situation you are in. It doesn't matter whom you are dealing with. Always remember, you have certain rights.

- YOU HAVE THE RIGHT TO HAVE YOUR OWN OPINION.

- YOU HAVE THE RIGHT TO BE LISTENED TO.

- YOU HAVE THE RIGHT TO BE TREATED WITH RESPECT.

- YOU HAVE THE RIGHT TO SAY WHAT YOU FEEL AND THINK IN A RESPECTFUL MANNER.

- YOU HAVE THE RIGHT TO ASK QUESTIONS.

You can develop an assertive communication style, but changing habits takes time. You can't make a complete shift overnight. So practice a little each day. Spend a few minutes thinking about your feelings or practicing your body language in front of a mirror. Ask your parents to work with you on some "I" statements. Really listen when your friends talk to you. Find small situations in which you can try out your new skills. Keep these ten steps in mind and work with them:

- **STEP 1: A "YOU VIEW"**
- **STEP 2: KNOW WHEN**
- **STEP 3: FOCUS ON FEELINGS**
- **STEP 4: "I" STATEMENTS**
- **STEP 5: SPEAK WITH CONFIDENCE**
- **STEP 6: BODY LANGUAGE**
- **STEP 7: LEARN TO LISTEN, LISTEN TO LEARN**
- **STEP 8: CONTROL YOUR TEMPER**
- **STEP 9: ACCEPT RESPONSIBILITY**
- **STEP 10: TAKE YOUR TIME**

Remember, if you follow these steps, you will become a successful assertive communicator. You'll have the tools to make strong friendships and end conflicts positively. With assertive communication, everyone wins!

GLOSSARY

aggressive forceful; ready to attack; able to harm

assertive able to be strong and clear

body language the way a person moves or holds himself or herself that communicates to other people

communication the exchange of thoughts, words, and information

communicator someone who shares thoughts, words, and information

conflicts strong disagreements or fights

ecstatic extremely happy; overjoyed

frustrated to feel blocked from doing something; to feel discouraged or not successful

misunderstandings situations in which someone cannot correctly understand another person

opinions a person's beliefs in or thoughts about something

options choices; possibilities

passive accepting situations without objecting to them

promotes helps in doing something; increases the possibility of something happening

rehearse to practice something; to prepare for an act or performance

relationships connections between people who are related to each other or have dealings with each other

resent to feel anger or bitter toward someone

situations the way things are; conditions

BOOKS

Berry, Joy Wilt. *Be Assertive.* PowerHouse Books

George, Abe. *Speak Right Up: Public Speaking Training Program of Young Speakers Club.* American Media House

Havelin, Kate. *Assertiveness: "How Can I Say What I Mean?"* Capstone

Palmer, Pat. *The Mouse, the Monster and Me: Assertiveness for Young People.* Uplift Press

WEB SITES

BAM! Body and Mind
www.bam.gov/sub_yourlife/yourlife_conflict.html
This interactive site is chock full of games and information about good mental health, including this site for resolving conflicts.

Kids' Health
www.cyh.com/HealthTopics/HealthTopicDetailsKids.aspx?p=335&np=287&id=2411
A fun and informative site to help children become more assertive

Resilient Kids
www.embracethefuture.org.au/kids/index.htm?getting_along.asp
An excellent site for exploring feelings and developing social skills like assertive communication

Slim Goodbody
www.slimgoodbody.com
Discover loads of fun and free downloads for kids, teachers, and parents.

INDEX

Aggressive communication 7, 10–11, 14, 15, 16

Anger 5, 9, 10, 15, 17, 18, 19, 22, 25

Arguing 17, 25

Assertive communication 5, 7, 12–13, 14, 15, 16, 23, 24–25, 26, 28, 29
Benefits of 13

Blame 20, 26

Body language 23, 27, 29

Borrowing 4, 22

Bullying 10, 11

Changing habits 29

Communication styles 6–12, 16

Confidence 23, 29

Conflicts 9, 12, 13, 29

Feelings 4, 5, 6, 8, 9, 10, 13, 18, 19, 20, 21, 22, 24, 26, 27, 28, 29

Friends 4, 10, 18, 21, 29

Frustration 5, 22

Habits 7

Happiness 18, 19

"I" statements 20–22, 27, 29

Identifying feelings 18–19, 21, 22

Interrupting 25

Listening 12, 24, 25, 28, 29

Name calling 21

Needs 5, 6, 8, 9, 13, 21, 28

Opinions 6, 11, 12, 16, 17, 28

Passive communication 6, 7, 8–9, 14, 15, 16

Peacekeeping 8

Questions 28

Rehearsing 27

Relationships 6, 13

Respect 12, 13, 15, 24, 26, 28

Responsibility, accepting 26, 29

Rights 5, 10, 13, 28

Sadness 18, 23

Shock 19

Speaking 11, 23, 28, 29

Styles 6

Teasing 22

Temper, control of 25, 29

Vocabulary for feelings 19, 21

Writing 19, 27

About the Author

John Burstein (also known as Slim Goodbody) has been entertaining and educating children for over thirty years. His programs have been broadcast on CBS, PBS, Nickelodeon, USA, and Discovery. He has won numerous awards including the Parent's Choice Award and the President's Council's Fitness Leader Award. Currently, Mr. Burstein tours the country with his multimedia live show "Bodyology." For more information, please visit **slimgoodbody.com**.